TOTALLY GOOFY:
The Republican Agenda, Today

By

Jim Green

DEDICATED TO:

THE TRUTH…..and in the age of Fake News "the truth", we have learned, is at a perilous risk! For some, the truth is critical—they understand that we cannot make accurate decisions—which impact our lives daily—without accurate information about a problem, and how we can accurately solve it---and yet, for one of our major TV networks lying is policy—and with the *intent* to deceive their viewers with the "Totally Goofy" Republican agenda! To illustrate, as we learned re Brian Williams….when he even shaded the truth at NBC, he was fired….at FAUX he would have been promoted…..i.e., in the nuclear age we simply cannot over-stress the danger of the adverse impact of pernicious propaganda—perhaps our most serious problem, today…..particularly, when we have a president who can't get from the beginning of a sentence, to the end--without lying…..

ISBN-10: 1545441359

ISBN-13: 978-1545441350

PROLOGUE

Several years back I submitted a question to "Ask Marilyn", in the Sunday Magazine "Parade"—[May 21, 2006—and as relevant today, as then] but not really expecting that she would answer...according to the Guinness Book of World Records, Marilyn vos Savant has the highest recorded IQ [ever], and my question was:

"It is obvious that our country is deeply divided: almost 50-50, judging. from the last election. Neither side sees any merit whatsoever in the programs of the other, and each side-is convinced that the other side has the dumbest ideas that ever came down the pike. Why are the two sides so far apart?"

Without getting too deep into the weeds, I really wasn't crazy about her answer....but leave to the reader to judge for themselves...she was pretty much saying that since our politicians weren't shooting at each other that this evidenced a certain "civility" [see her response, herein]....

I would only add, here, that the million woman march the day following Trump's inauguration--to protest his election--reflects a certain discontent with the current Republican ideology…..

And Trump's assertion that the largest crowds in America history came to DC just to see him-- at his inauguration [a patent lie]—was a dead-ringer that we are in an ideological wasteland…..Indeed, in just a short month Trump has the rest of the world convinced that he is loose cannon----

Trump has time to redeem himself—but it is questionable if he has the psychic makeup to do so…the big money says….NOPE…..

One of the ironies in this election, however, is that in alienating almost everyone---Trump also appeared to be a champion to our disenchanted [and our racists—his largest faction]—

And it may well be that this cobbled together faction is what led to Trump's election--albeit the possibility of Russian intrusion, and even vote flipping is still out—the investigations are just now getting under way…..

After his election, however, Trump took a severe turn to the right…at the expense of his "working class" populism—a fact which his cobbled together faction is slowly catching on to….[and Trump's approval has dipped to 35% in just over a month---the lowest for a new president in American history]!

But I drift…..and the purpose of this book is to re-visit my question to Marilyn…..and hopefully do a credible job at answering the question: "Why are the two sides so far apart?"

First, I like to post my opinions on FACEBOOK…..and I make no secret, whatsoever, that I am a Democrat [I am at a loss why _anyone_ would vote Republican]—but the minute it becomes known that I am a Democrat—the "Anti-Choice" folk come racing out of the woodwork to call me a "baby killer"----

An observation only an _insufferable jerk_ could come up with [I lost a child to a lung illness]—but to the person these _jerks_ vote Republican—Roe v Wade is about women having constitutional rights over their life—and only a fascist could miss the point—but I point this out to draw a stark difference between Democrats and Republicans, today!

Incidentally, there is _no_ "pro-life" group in America….and henceforth should be called the "anti-choice" faction---if these folks were pro-life they would support pre-natal and post-natal care for these children--—and they would be standing in line to adopt them—_none of which is included in their pernicious agenda_!

Further, they would be opposed to the death penalty and war….while most "and as good Republicans" embrace these dark [fascist] beliefs!

Also, almost to the person, Democrats are on one side of this issue, Republicans on the other—and with all due respect to Marilyn—the parties are at a stark difference to each other….

And to point out even more of our differences…..In just the past week Trump has signed an Executive Order erasing _all_ of the EPA protections supported by President Obama [and clearly in large part to pander to his racist faction]---and under the specious claim that this will create jobs—it is PURE BS [more later]!

Another contrast…..Republicans love to assert "American Exceptionalism."….but when someone tells me they are "exceptional"—I see "loser" written on their forehead—and in my experience, persons who are truly exceptional *never* go about telling others—indeed, to the contrary they are modest to a fault—

Further, It is great to think America is great—but *saying* we are "exceptional"—is saying to the rest of the world "you are not"—the term is comparative, by definition—and in many respects—particularly in our healthcare—<u>*WE ARE NOT!*</u>

In designing the healthcare system for South Korea—the experts used America for what *NOT TO DO*.......and we are 37th in the world in quality of healthcare, according to the World Health Organization......

And, in this regard—it is another example to contrast the difference between Democrats and Republicans, to wit:

Most Democrats support "single payer"—universal healthcare, Medicare for all, etc., ---it is seen as a "human right"—and a position held by every other major industrial country in the world!

In sharp contrast, most Republicans support a "for profit" market-driven healthcare—that exists no where else on Earth! Indeed, making a "profit" from a child's illness—defies negative adjectives to describe! And perhaps as a means to illustrate how money has corrupted America—in fact, the latter is the type of healthcare system we have in America, today!

And, we need look no further than the death threats every politician gets to understand the emotion aroused by differing political ideologies—at least on one level…..nevertheless, as it turned out Marilyn made it her lead item, with the heading "Are Republicans and Democrats really so far apart ideologically"—specifically, she responded:

> "You share a perception that is common, but I disagree with it. I think that the two major parties are almost alike. That's why our country is so successful, so stable and so peaceful. The parties hand the reins back and forth to each other with little more that smiles and tears at their election headquarters. New and former members of Congress pack up and move to new homes or back to their old ones. Joke writers

work overtime. The U.S. is a great place to live, work and complain."

A long-time friend, Robert Bohmfalk, ran for State Representative, District 44. in Texas in the 2016 election, and on September 30, 2016, our local paper published his observations about the Republican agenda, today—which mirrors virtually EVERY informed voter—and is particularly chilling because he suggests these things will happen "if" Trump is elected......and we all know the sad end of that tale.....

For the most part, Robert's observations apply to the pernicious Republican agenda, today—that adversely impacts *everyone*.....and with the exception of "14", which relates to Texas Republicans who want Texas to secede from the union [and with tongue in cheek, many would say Adios]---- but, in fact—for most of the past 100 years Democrats have dominated Texas—it was only when electronic voting machines, and vote flipping came along that Republicans started winning.....maybe just a coincidence......but to add to Bob's excellent insight will note with a **:

"1. BAN ALL BIRTH CONTROL.
Conservative pro-Life Republicans associate

birth control with abortion. One cannot be pro-Life and support birth control. They oppose Abstinence Plus Sex Education, and want to shut down Planned Parenthood. (Yes, we didn't think they would ban abortion with no exceptions either).

"2. END BACKGROUND CHECKS FOR GUN SALES. The NRA won this battle. Terrorist, criminals, gangs, domestic abusers, mentally ill, and minors will be allowed to purchase guns. Expect more mass shootings.

"3. END HEALTH CARE FOR WOMEN AND CHILDREN. Republicans will continue to repeal the Affordable Care Act with nothing to replace it with. They believe Capitalism is compatible with health care.

**As we all know now the Republicans were unable to repeal/replace the ACA—but no matter how this ends, there is one indisputable fact: Those who think like Republican Speaker Paul Ryan—that it is OK to knock 24 million off of healthcare, so the Republicans can give the 1% a $300 billion fluff gift—is an INSUFFERABLE JERK, a miserable excuse for a human being—a bottom-feeder scumbag— defies negative adjectives to describe!

"4. NO IMMIGRATION REFORM EVER.
They also oppose the Dream Act and Pathway to
Citizenship. Their only response is mass
deportation of 12 million people. They will not
compromise with the Democrats, always crying
"No Amnesty".

**It is "our frightened ones" who dwell on this
issue—which Trump played like a violin—the
same as our racists—the worst of us humans,
not Americans of quality…..

"5. IMPOSE ANTI- LGBT MOSAIC LAW.
They often quote from the first 5 Books of the
Old Testament, called Mosaic Law. They choose
Old Testament Fear and Hate over New
Testament Christian Love and Hope. They
oppose the Separation of Church and State.
They call it "religious freedom" to justify their
hatred and bigotry.

**For this faction, and like Pence…."Religious
Freedom" is the legalization of bigotry…..

"6. PRIVITIZE PUBLIC SCHOOLS. They plan
to again lay off thousands more teachers
resulting in over-crowded classrooms. They will

end all teacher unions. Some will remove Science and History classes.

**The potential for this coming true—based on what Trump has already done…..is chilling

"7. END SOCIAL SECURITY, MEDICARE, AND MEDICAID. They believe people will use savings accounts.

**Trump claims he will not tamper with Social Security and Medicare—but since he is currently unable to get from the beginning of a sentence to the end without lying—who knows, but one thing Trump does know is that he will have a war on his hands if he tries…..

"8. END LABOR UNIONS AND WORK CONDITIONS. They also want to end minimum wage, 8hr work day/40hr work week, overtime pay, sick pay, maternity leave, work safety regulations, and equal pay. They side with employers over employees.

**This is so true, and this erosion has been underway since WW II—since this issue is only of the *HIGHEST PRIORITY*, today, will take editorial license to expand briefly—to deal with the etiology of this issue: WORK is the right to be a productive member of the society one is born into—a given in primitive societies, but lost in the Age of Industrialization—for Americans, and driven by GREED, American employees have come to be seen as A POOL OF SLAVES: To Be Used And Discarded "at will" [Amazon/Kindle]—as we drifted further and further from the indispensable [here], and operative word "right". To illustrate, since WW II [and to this day] the Koch brothers--a metaphor, and fact, for the 1%--have spent hundreds of millions buying governors, legislators, Congress—with the specific intent to cement "at will" employment law in EVERY state [only Montana restricts to probationary employees], and to destroy our labor unions, i.e., to eliminate the protections for the American employee set forth in the Wagner Act [1935]. It has yet to be discussed but there is a *law* that controls the adverse impact unemployment has on market income—it is unavoidable—it is fact--the reason it isn't discussed is another book for another day—but it being hidden is in the same genre as world travel was out of the question when consensus had it that the world was flat...I call it the D/UE LAW [Diminished income to the market resulting from UE—unemployment]—and discussed variously, herein.....

"9. END THE ENVIROMENTAL PROTECTION AGENCY. They will put clean air and water at risk. They will ignore climate change, i.e, are climate change deniers.

"10. SEIZE MILLIONS OF GUNS, HOMES, CARS, AND PROPERTY from millions of law abiding undocumented Americans as they attempt to deport them. They will ignore the 4th Amendment and 10th Commandment. This will make America a Police State.

"11. GIVE TAX CUTS TO THE WEALTHY. They believe the wealthy should not have to share the cost or pay their fair share of taxes.

**This fraud, perpetrated on the American people, started with Reagan's Supply Side—and it is the Republican agenda to this day—and adding insult to injury, the Republican call it "tax reform"—what a joke! And compounding their "big lie"—their claim is that this will create jobs—but in fact, under Bush II— Americans lost jobs at the rate of 700,000 a month—as a *DIRECT* result of Supply Side…See "SUPPLY-SIDE REFRIED", Amazon/Kindle.

"12. NO COMPROMISE WITH DEMOCRATS EVER. There are no moderate Republicans . The Tea Party will put up a primary opponent to any Republican that compromises with Democrats.

"13. HAVE WARS FOUGHT BY DRAFTEES. They want to bring back the military draft which will include women. They did not learn the Vietnam War lesson about using draftees to fight our wars.

"14. HAVE TEXAS SECEDE FROM AMERICA. Many want to commit Treason by having Texas secede from America."

I hope you now understand why this book is titled TOTALLY GOOFY…..

A few closing comments in the Prologue—As Oscar Wilde averred "The only truly worthless opinion is an unbiased one"—so bias, agreed— but always in the interest in getting at the larger goal—the truth….

Incidentally, I published my first book on my 78th birthday [I am currently 82]—and not that I write that fast, or well—the materials were all there for the better part of the past 30 years, give or take, gathering dust—it was just a matter of pulling them together in some order—also, don't believe any book should be over 60 pages, plus/minus— i.e., can be read in the crapper--two hours, max--lol—but it seems best summed up by a very astute observer [wish I could recall their name to give credit]: Persons who write do so because they have no choice [it is a compulsion, an addiction..]—they become an "author", however, when people start reading what they have written….

Finally, a note to the reader—the papers and letters are not in sequence, and apologize for redundancy [please look for the nuggets…Thx--lol]—also, if you are a "typo-wonk"—are more concerned with sentence structure, etc., than content—you probably won't like my writing—and you will find a wayward capital letter, here and there, and appearing out of place and used for emphasis—or a missing page…Hey, I'm and Indie….I chalk most up to editorial license and tongue-in-cheek, self-effacing humor—so apologies, here—[I seriously support: Take what you do seriously, but never yourself….]….

Just look for content, please….THX

CHAPTER ONE

President Trump/Council of Economic Advisers:

The market is ideal at producing and selling corn flakes and cars…..it is miserable at Job Creation, and Health Care….

The operative word for the market is making a "profit", and cutting costs/services is intrinsic to this end…..

First, the idea of making a "profit" off of an ill child—or anyone's illness for that matter defies negative adjectives to define…..

And the 1% has spent hundreds of millions since WW II buying governors/legislators to abolish Employee Rights, and our labor unions in America—[When it is critical to survival of the market in a 21st Century economy—to celebrate, rather than condemn, Humphrey-Hawkins]….

Specifically to cement "at will" employment in every state [only Montana limits to probationary employees]---and the implementation of corrupt union busting "right to work" laws—

And solely in the interest of **PURE GREED** [devoid of any socially redeeming value]!

Given automation, alone, we have had excessive unemployment over 70% of the time since 1980 [twice that of preceding years]—and running in parallel with a louder and louder voice from the electorate for "JOBS, JOBS, JOBS"—

But it is foolish to look to the market to create these jobs—with the proliferation of robots the further we advance into the 21st Century, replacing human work—i.e., and when the objective of the market is to eliminate jobs to increase profits!

And, Job Creation relying on the archaic **BELIEF/OXYMORON** that "the market can provide anybody wanting a job, with a job" [which is **PURE BS**]—has resulted in an unemployment rate below 3% only ONCE since WW II—in 1953—leaving millions jobless in its wake—and created an epidemic of gun violence in our inner-cities!

It would be ideal if the market could provide all the jobs we need—and the truth is, we have a blended economic system—and the two components are, in fact, indispensable to each other:

Social Insurance is a vital ingredient in building a vibrant and decent society—And, invent a better widget, sell the company for a million bucks, and retire in Florida [capitalism]—is as well a vital ingredient in building a vibrant and decent society.

Ref: HR 1000; The D/UE LAW: The Massive Loss of Market Income, Resulting From The Lack of Employment, and FULL EMPLOYMENT IS A PRO-MARKET CONCEPT, Amazon/Kindle

Jim Green, Democrat candidate for Congress, 2000

Thank you for contacting the White House.

CHAPTER TWO

President Obama/Presidential Innovation Fellows:

Since WW II our single method of Job Creation in America has been based on the belief/propaganda that "The market can provide anybody wanting a job, with a job"……

And when it didn't work--we pretended it did, and drifted into Santa Clause-like wishful thinking—asserting "it is the American way", or "God's will"—or some such lie we told ourselves--as rational Job Creation, in a changing world, drifted further and further away…..

For instance, this method of Job Creation has not resulted in a UE rate below 3% since 1953, but we limped along—terrorized by McCarthyism, and leaving millions jobless—and by the mid-1970's the colliding forces of globalization, automation, technology reached critical mass, resulting in a cosmic shift in the world economy—with subsequent "High and persistent unemployment pervasive throughout the OECD since the mid-1970's", according to

Dr. William F. Mitchell, and every credible economist.

And, going forward the data got even more grim—i.e., since 1980 we have had excessive UE 70% of the time [twice that of preceding years], and by the Crash of 2008—8 million were rendered jobless—[and in spite of an extremely anemic recovery we inched down from 10% to 5% UE, inexplicably still relying on the above method]—---

And with the result that by the September 2016 DOL Jobs Report, we still have 8 million Americans looking for work, that can't find any…..and in an economy limping along on a flat tire—as a direct result of high UE, and a Republican Congress determined to sabotage America—for political reasons--

The lesson is: Our choices are adapt and change in a world that is changing—whether we like it or not—or be forced to create a Police State to hold in place antiquated and unworkable laws and policies [in this case re our Job Creation]—and sadly, America has opted for the latter—and we need look no further than the police marching in lock-step in Charlotte, this past week, as proof!

The flaw in all of this is based on simple common sense: "The mechanic can't fix the engine without the proper tools"—and when Jobs, Jobs, Jobs is the major mantra in this election—fixing unemployment is hopeless so long as we insist on a method of Job Creation—THAT DOESN'T WORK!

Proposed Solutions: HR 1000, and FULL EMPLOYMENT IS A PRO-MARKET CONCEPT, Amazon

Jim Green, Democrat opponent to Lamar Smith, 2000

Thank you for contacting the White House!

CHAPTER THREE

Editor: NY TIMES

Capitalism is ideal in producing and selling corn flakes and cars—It doesn't work in solving "social problems" such as unemployment and our healthcare....

And when we have tried "privatization" to solve our social problems—it has been a disaster:

Specifically, essential programs have been cut—such as the elimination of text books from the Job Corps education program—to increase profits, and cronyism has run rampant—

And in our "for profit" healthcare system, billions of dollars are siphoned away from the premiums we send in—and do not go to the healthcare of ANYONE—but rather is used to pay for lobbyists, to make the CEO's filthy rich—and spent on propaganda ads to keep it that way!

Additionally, President Obama had a weapon in 2009, not available to FDR: Were it not for the $800 billion in Social Security Insurance moneys percolating up through our economy annually, ie., in 2008—we would not be talking about having narrowly averted another Great Depression—We would be buried in one!

The truth is, we have a blended economic system—and the two components are, in fact, indispensable to each other:

Social Insurance is a vital ingredient in building a vibrant and decent society—And, invent a better widget, sell the company for a million bucks, and retire in Florida [capitalism]—is as well a vital ingredient in building a vibrant and decent society.

So why do we have this war of words pitting the two against each other—rather than educating the American people regarding the indispensable symbiotic relationship they have to each other?

Were it not for the $2 trillion + Washington infuses back into the economy annually—capitalism would fold in a NY Second!

And yet, most Republicans ask God in their prayers at night to be protected from communists, or socialists, or even worse "liberals"—[i.e., monsters under their bed] with "liberal" henceforth to be replaced with the word "Christian".....

Regarding "unemployment" [hereafter UE]—it is essential that we evolve, and given "automation", alone, in our 21st Century economy we need to look upon UE the same as we look upon Cancer, Polio, or AIDS, as a ubiquious disease—a menace to society, in need of eradication....via [15 USC § 3101]—which would restrict our UE to 3%, permanently!

Best regards,

Jim Green

CHAPTER FOUR

President Obama:

It is impossible to reform our broken criminal justice system—absent our creating a viable job creation program in America.

And while it is generally believed that we do have a job creation program, in fact, we do not!

We have the BELIEF that "the market can provide anybody wanting a job, with a job"— but the data shows that only ONCE since WW II has minority unemployment in our inner-cities, with drug economies, and an epidemic of homicides [i.e., not fixing unemployment has turned our inner-cities into war zones, and created a breeding ground for our inexplicable incarceration rate].

Further this "belief" has been a stumbling block in finding a solution for our pervasive unemployment--In short, we have not been looking for a solution—because our policy makers believe we have one—and apparently few have looked at thc data....

Also, ignored in the discussion this belief resulted in an unemployment rate below 3%--in 1953—leaving millions jobless in its wake-- and has resulted in:

60% is that unemployment is a "social" problem, with adverse, and oft severe social consequences—both for the individual, as well as the larger society [i.e., it is the responsibility of the larger society to solve]—

With tentacles integral to all of the social problems facing Americans, today—for instance, ending unemployment is integral to Criminal Justice Reform, and the repair of our crumbling infrastructure....

Further, in 1975 we spent $5 educating our youth, for every $1 we spent on prisons.....by the mid-1990's [with the American people having been terrorized by the Willie Horton ad—and on an hysterical prison building spree] our competing tax dollars tipped in favor of prisons—and at present we spend more on prisons, than on educating our youth.

The irony in all of this is that we have the "legal authorization", on the books to reduce our unemployment rate to 3%, tomorrow [15 USC §

3101—and deficit-neutral HR 1000, currently in Committee]—and also ignored in this context, is that President Obama had a weapon in addressing our economic meltdown in 2008, not available to FDR—and that is the $800 billion in Social Security Insurance claims percolating up through our economy—and in the absence of which--We would be buried in another Great Depression!

Turning the page—and given "automation", alone, is critical going forward in the 21st Century—and is a "win-win"—the American people win, and the market wins....

Ref: FULL EMPLOYMENT IS A PRO-MARKET CONCEPT, Amazon

Jim Green, Democrat opponent to Lamar Smith, 2000

CHAPTER FIVE

President Obama/Council of Economic Advisers:

Our network of market-driven economics [the OECD, including the U.S]—currently have a pernicious job creation modality—with resulting high and pervasive unemployment since the mid-1970's—and on a collision course with the future—i.e., given "automation", alone, fewer and fewer jobs are being created with each passing year, as we advance into the 21st Century....

This job creation modality is based on the erroneous propaganda/belief that "the market can provide anybody wanting a job, with a job"—and yet, only ONCE since WW II has this modality resulted in an unemployment rate below 3%--in 1953—leaving millions jobless in its wake, and has resulted in our inner-cities turning into war zones--with 60% minority unemployment, drug economies, and an epidemic of homicides.

The irony in this disaster, however, is that the U.S. correctly anticipated this result in 1978—

and provided the American people with a solution, i.e., the "legal authorization" [15 USC § 3101] to limit our unemployment henceforth to "3%", and as we advance into the 21st Century—

With a ton of cash poured into our political system, and a mind-set with both feet planted on the plantation—--special interests sabotaged this law to prevent its implementation—to the detriment of Americans, and America [ISIS is the least of our worries in America, when we have the Republican party]!

Unemployment is a "social" problem, with adverse social consequences....it is solely the province of the larger society to solve—and leaving the solution to anything as erratic as the market—as we do now—is patently absurd!

The bottom line is that unemployment is a NO ONE WINS....the jobless lose, civility loses, and the market loses, to wit:

THE LAW OF DIMINISHED INCOME TO THE MARKET FROM UNEMPLOYMENT [hereafter D/UE LAW]

3% is the zero-sum threshold above which unemployment triggers diminished labor training and skills, under-utilizing capital resources, reducing the rate of productivity advance, increasing unit labor costs, reducing the general supply of goods and services--and the loss in income to the Market is compounded exponentially with each percentage point of increase in unemployment, above 3%.

Ref: HR 1000 [in Committee], and FULL EMPLOYMENT IS A PRO-MARKET SOLUTION, Amazon

Jim Green, Democrat opponent to Lamar Smith, 2000

Thank You!

Thank you for contacting the White House

CHPATER SIX

THE HISTORY OF HOW WE GOT WHERE WE ARE
[WW II to Present]

Following WW II, President Truman signed into law the [FULL] EMPLOYMENT ACT of 1946, to provide employment for our returning troops.

Ironically, half-way around the world, Australia codified into their law an almost identical Bill, and for the same reason—

Difference is—Australia actually put their law into effect, and over the next 30 years it was intrinsic to employment policy in Australia that "anybody wanting to work should be able to find a job"—and save for a brief recession in 1961/62 their unemployment was 2%, or less. This period is still referred to as their "Golden Age", in Australia.

Unforeseen by either country, however, in the mid-1970's the world economy underwent a major paradigm shift as a result of the colliding forces of automation, globalization, technology, etc., reaching a critical mass—in brief, an adjustment towards modernity—From a perverse perspective, we became victims of our success....

The instability caused by this transition, however, resulted in a malaise, and ushered in the ill-winds of greed-driven neo-liberalism with its indifference to unemployment, and the likes of Thatcher and Reagan—and the menace of this greed-driven agenda was exploded by Bush II, resulting in obscene disparities in wealth that persists, and is the cause of much friction between right and left, to this day.

It also ushered in high and pervasive unemployment throughout our market-driven economies, the OECD—with 6% unemployment in Australia now the norm, and double-digit unemployment common throughout the Eurozone, to this day.

As a result of the "malaise", however, the U.S. took an aggressive, pro-active role in addressing the, above, economic shift—and in 1978 President Carter signed into law one of the most important laws in the 20th Century--an expansion of President Truman's full employment, i.e., Pro-Market 15 USC § 3101--which provides a *"legal authorization"* to create a "reservoir of public employees" [*indispensable to the effective functioning of a 21st Century market economy*]--at any time our unemployment in America exceeds "3%"—

But in spite of 3% unemployment being the threshold point above which unemployment starts substantially undermining the Market—this *legal authorization* has never been implemented--

And in spite of deficit-neutral HR 1000, or The Neighbor-To-Neighbor Job Creation Act—A federally mandated Social Insurance, owned by our employed, to provide a fund to hire/train our unemployed—[more on the critical need to apply this job creation methodology in a 21st Century market economy, ahead]….

Ref: FULL EMPLOYMENT IS A PRO-MARKET CONCEPT, Amazon/Kindle

Jim Green, Democrat opponent to Lamar Smith, Congress, 2000

CHAPTER SEVEN

THE HISTORY OF HOW WE GOT WHERE WE ARE

[Mid-1970's to Present]

In the mid-1970's, the colliding forces of automation, technology, globalization, etc., reached a critical mass—resulting in a Market no longer capable of producing the jobs necessary to its viability, and causing ubiquitous unemployment in all of the OECD countries—and leaving their leaders conflicted, ever since, regarding the displaced employee. Eurozone unemployment is still in double digits, and Greece and Spain both in excess of 20%, plus. High unemployment was also a major factor in Arab Spring.

In the U.S., we took a pro-active role in addressing this economic shift—and in 1978 President Carter signed into law 15 USC § 3101- -which "authorizes" the creation of a "reservoir of public employment" at any time our unemployment in America exceeds "3%".

In 1979, however, and in a panic over Humphrey-Hawkins—our ultra-conservative foundations, and desperate to promote the Supply-Side fraud, embraced a flawed paper by an obscure MIT student, David L. Birch "The Job Generation Process"; and [with lots of cash] gave his paper biblical importance, and every president since has cited his finding as gospel.

Birch's paper concluded that "small businesses" were the greatest generator of new jobs—problem is, for the purposes of policy-making—it is BS. In a study at Harvard University in 2010, "The Myth of Small Business Job Creation" The research shows "no systematic relationship between firm size and growth." And that small businesses can actually detract from job growth.

In spite of this, however, Washington struggles, still, to make this antiquated notion, work--that it is only the market that can create jobs—and the result has been a disaster, politically as well as otherwise!

It would be impossible to still have 7.8% unemployment—if we were on the right path—

and among other problems with this concept--if the market fails, the unemployed are out of luck.

Further, unemployment is a "social" problem we are seeking to address with a highly unstable, incompatible entity: The Market

What apparently isn't clear going forward is that an expanding and contracting public workforce is an *indispensable* component to the *effective* functioning of a modern market economy—

The market thrives when we have a robust, employed, consuming workforce—and overlooked is that HR 1000 [currently in Committee], and the proposed "Neighbor-To-Neighbor Job Creation Act" www.Inclusivism.org [both authorized under Humphrey-Hawkins], are deficit-neutral--Pro-Market "win-win" solutions:

The American people win, and capitalism wins—

Jim Green, Democrat candidate for Congress, 2000

CHAPTER EIGHT

Friends: In the event you have gotten this far—according to the Federal Election Commission, I am a candidate for president in the 2016 election—and rest assured I am not delusional, or like Trump…on an ego trip…..I filed solely to deliver a message—you are reading it—and to urge passage of the above legislation….

To Whom It May Concern—in Washingon:

OUR CHOICES ARE: Adapt and change in a world that is changing, whether we like it or not, OR be forced to create a Police State to hold our anachronistic policies, practices and laws in place—

And in America, today, we have chosen the latter…..and as only one pernicious example, of thousands—Ferguson is the result….

In a comedic, but religious context we hear of persons asking God for a sign—anything—which will warn us that we are on the wrong path, and need to change direction…..and our

Police State choice, above, is *our sign*…..few are listening….

To illustrate a critical area in which we need to adapt and change in a 21st Century economy: We have far more work that needs to be done in America, than we have persons to fill these jobs—And 86% of Americans believe that "Anybody wanting to work should be able to find a job"---So, why on earth *in a democracy*, do we have 9 million jobless Americans—[per the 11/14 DOL Jobs report]?

The answer is because our *method* of job creation in America is based on a Fairy Tale! Specifically, our current *one and only* job creation methodology in America, is based on the myth/sacred cow:

"The market can provide anybody wanting a job, with a job"—

Problem is—it is pure BS—and only *once* since WW II has this methodology resulted in an unemployment rate below 3%--in 1953 [i.e., which translates into 5 million left jobless]-- because the market *cannot* create enough jobs— in short, the jobs for this 5 million jobless--*don't exist*!

The right-wing propaganda mills trick our fools into believing that the market has created this 5 million jobs, but because those on welfare are "lazy and don't want to work" this 5 million jobs go unfilled—but that is *pure balderdash!*

The vast majority of persons on welfare, are there *because* the *market* cannot create enough jobs, i.e., the market lacks the viability to create these jobs—the jobs simply *do not exist*!

And as further proof, according to the CBO, on our current path it will be 2017 before America returns to even an anemic 5.5% unemployment rate [following the Great Recession] and if the market fails in the interim—the jobless are out of luck!

Further, this travesty is compounded because the Republicans cling to devious and discredited Supply Side Economics [to this day] as a solution, to wit:

Siphon America's wealth away from the consuming middle—give this windfall of cash to the Koch Bros [a metaphor for the 1%, hereafter "KB"]—they will build factories all across our fair land—everyone will have a job in the corporation—and we will all live happily ever after—Yes, folks it is a fairy tale!

And what we learned from this dark cloud over America is what Bush I called it long ago—before America was subjected to this devious scam—i.e., Supply-Side is "VooDoo Economics"!

So why have we allowed ourselves to be deceived by this Republican scam—[handcrafted by a plutocracy/oligarchy that still has one foot on the plantation]? But I don't want to giveaway the surprise ending—and some of my response isn't printable….! Further, and to say it up front….I am a capitalist—I support 100%: Build a better widget, sell it for a million bucks, and retire in South Florida….it is the Republican agenda, today, that is anti-market…more on this throughout…..

When President Carter handed the reigns over to Reagan in 1981—he left America with a very modest $60 billion deficit—as a direct result of Supply-Side, however, when Republicans held the White House [Clinton actually cut the deficit]—this $60 billion ballooned to a staggering $10 trillion by 2008—and it has cost

Americans an additional $7+trillion to clean up this Republican mess—

Ask any economist: Our only way out of a meltdown *is to buy our way out!* [it was the lesson learned from the Great Depression].

And anyone who thinks McCain, had he been elected, would not have addressed this with a Stimulus, the same as President Obama in 2009—is stuffed between the ears with rice pudding......

Further, we learned that we cannot siphon America's wealth away from the consuming middle, and give it to the "KB"—without sending our economy into meltdown—as occurred in 1987 and 2008—in short, the Supply-Side scam has a shelf-life of about 7 years before the economy collapses—and as noted, costing the taxpayers trillions to put a floor under a disappearing economy!

And another fallout/direct result from this dark chapter is the disparity in wealth it has created in America—AKA the "wealth gap"--and currently the "richest 1 percent in the United States now own more wealth than the bottom 90 percent"—the second highest in our history, the first was just before the Great Depression.

A couple of other factors that played into the above scenario—when every waking moment in capitalism is spent pondering how to eliminate as many of us humans, as possible, from the workplace—to increase "profits"—why, on Earth, would we look to the market to solve our unemployment crisis in America?

As well, few things on earth are more unstable than the market....we can count on one hand the number of corporations in America that were around in 1900....with tens of thousands long since disappeared; and given "automation", alone, the market will produce fewer and fewer jobs the further we advance into the 21st Century.

Further, unemployment is a "social" problem—we, as the larger society have the responsibility to solve—i.e., it is unrealistic to expect the market to solve this problem—the market is in the "for profit" business, not the social work business—and the former would not long be in business--if they were...for example, we should never condemn the CEO for closing a plant when they are losing money—but we should be outraged by a government that doesn't have a clue re the displaced employees…..

Also, unemployment is a *no one wins* …..the jobless lose, and market loses, to wit:

> 3% is the zero-sum threshold above which unemployment triggers diminished labor training and skills, under-utilizing capital resources, reducing the rate of productivity advance, increasing unit labor costs, and reducing the general supply of goods and services--and the loss in income to the Market is compounded exponentially with each percentage point of increase in unemployment, above 3%.

> Short Definition:

> 3% is the zero-sum threshold above which unemployment starts substantially undermining the Market--and the loss in income to the Market is compounded exponentially with each percentage point of increase in unemployment, above 3%.

In sum, our job creation should be based on: Fix unemployment, and this will fix the market [HR 1000], rather than [our current mind-set] Fix the market, and this in turn fix unemployment [HR 2847] – with a result that has been a disaster—as we inch along in our job recovery, see data above, and when we didn't *Fix Unemployment* a retaliatory electorate ushered in a House filled with lunatics in the 2010 election, and then doubled down in 2014!

Look around—all signs in our economy are up—and yet over two-thirds of our rank and file believe "we are moving in the wrong direction"—their perception is that our economy is in the tank—that we are in an economic malaise—a condition that would disappear overnight if we did, in fact, *Fix Unemployment*!

Best guess is that Congress passed, and President Obama signed into law HR 2847 [the HIRE Act], in 2009—which is based on fix the market, and this will fix unemployment [180 degrees off course]—but they did this because of the pervasive [but false] *belief* that "The market can provide anybody wanting a job, with a job"—it is *pure BS......it doesn't work*! Had we insisted on putting a lawnmower engine in the rocket to get us to the Moon....we would never have gotten there...[same difference]....and all of the empirical evidence is proof HR 2847 didn't create anywhere near the jobs needed...

Jim Green, Democrat opponent to Lamar Smith, Congress, 2000

CHAPTER NINE

HOPPER-READY: THE NEIGHBOR-TO-NEIGHBOR JOB CREATION ACT

[1] PROPOSED LEGISLATION:

THE NEIGHBOR-TO-NEIGHBOR JOB CREATION ACT

A Pro-Market, deficit-neutral, federally mandated, Social Insurance, owned by our employed, to provide a fund to hire/train our unemployed.

SECTION 1. SHORT TITLE.

This Act shall be cited as The Neighbor-To-Neighbor Job Creation Act [To establish employment/training opportunities for the unemployed in compliance with the "Legal Authorization" in Public Law 15 USC § 3101, for the creation of a "reservoir of public employees", anytime our unemployment rate exceeds "3%", with an emphasis on training for market needs, including a training stipend, where there is a shortage of trained workers--hereafter NTN].

SEC. 2. DEFINITIONS.

In this Act the following definitions apply:
    (1) SECRETARY- The term `Secretary' means the Secretary of Labor.
    (2) STATE- The term `State' has the meaning given such term in section 102(2) of the Housing and Community Development Act (42 U.S.C. 5302(2)).
    (3) TRUST FUND- The term `Trust Fund' refers to the Department of Labor Full Employment Trust Fund.
    (4) UNIT OF GENERAL LOCAL GOVERNMENT- The term `unit of general local government' has the meaning given such term in section 102(1) of the Housing and Community Development Act (42 U.S.C. 5302(1)).
    (5) URBAN COUNTY- The term `urban county' has the meaning given such term in section 102(6) of the Housing and Community Development Act (42 U.S.C. 5302(6)).
    (6) WEB SITE- The Secretary shall establish an Internet Web site to serve as

an information clearinghouse for job training and employment opportunities funded by the Trust Fund.

SEC. 3. EMPLOYMENT OPPORTUNITY GRANTS TO STATES, LOCAL GOVERNMENT.

(a) Use of Funds-A recipient of a grant under this section shall use the grant primarily for infrastructure repair, including, but not limited to:

(A) The painting and repair of schools, community centers, and libraries.
(B) The restoration and revitalization of abandoned and vacant properties to alleviate blight in distressed and foreclosure-affected areas of a unit of general local government.
(C) The augmentation of staffing in Head Start, child care, and other early childhood education programs to promote school readiness and early literacy.

(D) The renovation and enhancement of maintenance of parks, playgrounds, and other public spaces.

Respectfully Submitted,

Jim Green, Democrat candidate for Congress, Dist 21, TX, 2000

CHAPTER TEN

WHAT WE NEED TO DO GOING FORWARD IN THE 21ST CENTURY:

Inexplicably "public employment" is seen the same as WPA—where millions are employed directly by the federal government—when that model is not only outmoded—it is insufficient to address our problems in the 21st century.

What we need today is an expanding and contracting public workforce—that expands during downturns in the market, and contracts as employees return to the private sector [Google: The Buffer Stock Employment Model]—triggered anytime our unemployment exceeds "3%" [as "authorized" under Humphrey-Hawkins]--and least understood: This is an INDISPENSABLE component in the effective functioning of our 21st Century Market.

The market thrives when we have a robust, employed, consuming workforce—our manufacturers are sitting on $2 trillion in cash because they do not have consumers for their products—i.e., absent consumers, they lay off employees—[and the Republican solution, Reaganomics, has acted as an accelerate to this downward spiral—and which Romney promises to return us to if he is elected]!

In short, the above model is a "win-win" solution—the American people win, and capitalism wins!

To achieve this, what is being urged is "The Neighbor-To-Neighbor Job Creation Act": A federally mandated, mutual insurance—owned by our employed [from janitor to CEO] to create a fund to hire/train our unemployed.

To be viable, however, our job creation solution *MUST* contain:

1] Be based on the premise that we have far more work that needs to be done in America, than we have persons to fill these jobs.

2] It MUST have renewable funding.

3] It will not add a dime to our deficit.

To expand briefly, it is currently believed, erroneously, that we need "make work" jobs so that everyone who wants to work will have a job—but this is absurd—and an insult to "Yankee Ingenuity".

We do not have an unemployment crisis from a shortage of jobs, or money—but rather from a shortage of imagination.

Regarding "renewable funding" ALL of our job creation solutions, to date, have been based on the mind-set: "jump start" the market, and the market will in turn create all the jobs we need— and even setting aside that this is untrue, our current job creation is moving at a snail's pace—long past the unemployment benefits drying up—with the CBO projecting that even with the JOBS Act, signed into law on April 6, 2012--it will be 2017 before we return to a barely acceptable 5.5% unemployment rate!

Further, by its nature when we "jump start" -- the employment ends when the funding runs out as we learned from the Stimulus—whereas any real fix to our unemployment crisis _demands_ renewable funding....

And whether the electorate will accept an unemployment rate hovering around 8% on election day—is the $64,000 question....

Regarding not adding a dime to our deficit—under The Neighbor-To-Neighbor Job Creation Act [NTN], the *funding* to reduce our unemployment to 3% comes from an insurance owned by our employed, rather than added to our deficit—

If one is employed in America, participation in this insurance plan is mandatory—similar in concept to our auto insurance or Social Security Insurance [and without question the most successful social program in American history].

Jobs beget jobs--And with a modest policy cost of 4% of salary we can create more "private-sector" jobs in 6 months, that HR 2847, and the JOBS Act, in 6 years—and unlike these laws—NTN will not add a dime to our deficit!

Finally, this is in total concert with the will of the American people, i.e., that "anybody willing to work should be able to find a job"—and the American people have told our politicians time and again of their willingness to chip in to help their neighbor get a job [and as an *insurance*, as above, it also protects their continued employment]—it is just that Washington is deaf as an adder!

CHAPTER ELEVEN

President Obama/Council of Economic Advisers:

Public-Sector jobs strengthen our free-enterprise market economy—i.e., they are a critical component to the viability of our 21ˢᵗ Century economy--rather than weakening the market--as propagandist, with one foot on the plantation, fraudulently deceive the public into believing for the purposes of exploiting American employees…..

Indeed, since WW II, the Koch brothers [both literally, and a metaphor, here, for the 1%] have spent tens of millions buying governors and legislators, to cement "at will" employment in every state [and currently only Montana limits to probationary employees]; and to destroy "collective bargaining", i.e., unions in America—

In sum, they have spent tens of millions of dollars to destroy "employee rights" in America!

To understand the importance of "collective bargaining" for employees, it is informative to take a page from history:

When Hitler became the dictator in Germany, one of his first laws was to make it illegal for more than three persons to gather on the street—and German citizens were subject to immediate arrest if they did.

The same principal is being used by preventing employees putting their heads together, as it were, to bargain for employee rights—and recently one group of employees placed "job security" over a salary increase—with the irony being that the specific objective of "at will" employment—is to destroy "job security"!

In short, the deceptive propaganda to frighten Americans regarding "public-sector" jobs, has but a single parent: To exploit American labor—by some, to assuage deep-seated feelings of inferiority [they can only feel tall, by making others small, in their eyes]--—but most often for just pure GREED!

Where our policies makers go wrong by pandering to some in the oligarchy—and/or buying into this fraudulent propaganda:

Unemployment is a NO ONE WINS—the jobless lose, civility loses, and the market loses, to wit:

THE LAW OF DIMINISHED INCOME TO THE MARKET FROM UNEMPLOYMENT
[hereafter D/UE LAW]

Short Definition:

> **3% is the zero-sum threshold above which unemployment starts substantially undermining the Market--and the loss in income to the Market is compounded exponentially with each percentage point of increase in unemployment, above 3%.**

Ref: IT IS IMPOSSIBLE TO BE A CHRISTIAN, AND VOTE REPUBLICAN, Amazon

Jim Green, Democrat opponent to Lamar Smith, 2000

CHAPTER TWELVE

FAIL-SAFE ELECTRONIC VOTING

TO THE READER: Given you have gotten this far, and agree with the proposed changes—and particularly given the pernicious Citizens United—our democracy, and the above, or any, progress, will be in peril absent a "fail-safe" electronic voting system. The following is my proposed solution, and like every solution proposed, here, feed-back--your proposed improvement, etc. is welcomed:

THE FAIL-SAFE ELECTRONIC VOTING ACT

1) EVERY electronic voting machine (hereafter EVM), must be inexpensive, identical throughout the U.S. in a 1/150 ratio, and *must count and produce a hard-copy of the recorded votes*. In addition, an extra copy of their recorded votes would be produced (not necessarily a hard-copy), marked "Voter's Copy", and containing "NOTICE: Do Not Destroy Until Every Election On Your Ballot Is Certified". [If Wal-Mart handed us a piece of paper with the words "trust us" as a receipt for

our purchases—we would be outraged—and yet, this is our current electronic voting nightmare— but in this case it is our democracy at risk]!

2) *After confirming that their votes are recorded correctly*, the voter would then insert the hard-copy ballot into a software-free (count only) optical scanner (hereafter OS), for a second count. The hard-copy ballot would be retained by election officials in the event a candidate asks for a recount (***not possible under the current system, and which undermines the legality of each such election***). The EVM and the OS must be manufactured by different companies (which is universally true today).

3) Election officials assigned to oversee the EVM, would be prevented by law from overseeing the OS, and vice-versa, and stiff criminal penalties would be imposed for violations.

4) Further, every EVM would be programmed with raw data re the total registration rolls, by party, and norms for their voting history, etc.,----as an "alert" to a possible irregularity, such as an "under-vote"—or "vote-flipping" etc., and *standards* established to suspend certification where there is an "improbable result", at least

temporarily, of a particular election until the discrepancy is cleared up. (This is what computers do best, and it would be very easy to create such a program).

5) At the end of the election day, tallies would be taken from the EVM and the OS, for each candidate. *If the tallies didn't balance for any given election, or if there is an "alert", that election cannot be certified until the "error" is corrected.* If the candidates agree (the victory is certain), minor discrepancies in the count could be disregarded. While probably rare, the Voter, or a random sample of Voters, would be required by law to return their Copy of the recorded votes to the election office to clear up any "error", or where an "alert" signals the need for same.

6) Further, every state provides for a recount when the total vote falls below a certain percent of difference between the candidates, impossible to conduct with the current EVM. And thus Congress must mandate the following regarding presidential candidates: A RUN-OFF election is mandated and triggered in those states where the percent of total vote is less than .5% of difference between the two candidates; said election to be held on the second Saturday

following the election, on PAPER BALLOTS ONLY, and contain ONLY the names of the relevant candidates, for instance: "Barack Obama, Democrat" and "John McCain, Republican"—with oversight in counting by a representative(s) of each party—said procedure providing more than adequate time to meet the Electoral College mandate [Ideally, all of this could be eliminated if we did away with the Electoral College, but until then….]. NOTE: Had this been the law in 2000, Al Gore would be our president, and America would have been spared the economic, etc., disaster that followed!

7) Finally, absent the above safeguards, and until these safeguards are in place--Congress must mandate that PAPER BALLOTS, ONLY, can be used in our presidential elections. This is not a "partisan" issue, it is a "pro-democracy" issue. Most importantly, this will return the responsibility for our elections, and our vote counting, back into the hands of the individual voter, where it belongs, and out of the hands of "corporate control"---*it is after all "our democracy", itself, that is at risk if we don't take these steps---and in that regard, is there any time or cost differential that is too great?*

Jim Green

CHAPTER THIRTEEN

I didn't write the following. It is a cut and paste from FACEBOOK, or some blog [would like to give credit if knew the author]--but it is so on target regarding how "fear" is driving Conservative policy in America today—i.e., is undermining America and our progress—and relegating America to a Third World country status, rather than a world leader—FDR had it on the nose in "All we have to fear, is fear itself"…at his inaugural in 1933….

"Conservatives are such cowards: they are afraid of gay people getting married or serving in the military; they are afraid of bringing terrorists to super max prisons in the US from which no one has ever escaped; they are afraid of the boy scouts letting gay kids in; they are afraid of everyone voting and are constantly suppressing the vote under some bogus voter fraud theory; they are afraid of letting students vote at their universities; they are afraid of women having the right to choose; they even are afraid of women getting contraception [the real issue actually is a women's agency and control over their bodies]; they are afraid of immigration reform leading to citizenship because they are afraid of-- name whatever reason; they are afraid of mandating gun purchasers to undergo background checks for crazy people and terrorists; they are afraid of people smoking pot; they are afraid of climate change being real and contradicting their beloved Bible; they are afraid of legitimate campaign reform; they are afraid of Muslims; they are afraid of blacks; they are afraid of atheists; they are afraid of hippies; they are afraid of socialists; they are probably still afraid of monsters under their beds; they are just rank cowards and keep making things up to be afraid of."

CHAPTER FOURTEEN

[I couldn't resist including this…and yes I am the author…..]

A MESSAGE FROM GOD

MANY CENTURIES AGO, a man of the cloth, we don't know his name, and in a flash of insight (perhaps induced by peyote) told his flock that "sex is a sin". And lo and behold he learned that by taking a very natural and healthy part of our life and turning it into something that was "dirty and nasty", that he could imprison his flock, and fill his coffers, and hallelujah it was a great day for the Lord!

Quickly, his miracle spread to other churches in his village, and then to the next village, and then the next county, and then state, and soon it spread to all the churches in the ancient world, and all of their flocks cowed in fear and shame and became imprisoned, and their coffers over-floweth. Hallelujah, it was a great day for the Lord!

And to keep the myth alive they started inventing stories, half-baked stories, that made no sense to anyone who is rational, such as "Mary was a virgin"—well, she just had to be a virgin because she would never partake in anything that was dirty and nasty, like sex (if you're doing it right), and this was necessary to make "sex is a sin" make sense...so they invented a Mary that was "sinless"--you get the picture. And their coffers over-floweth. Hallelujah, it was a great day for the Lord!

No one seemed to be bothered that when we play tricks on the human mind by taking something that is very natural and healthy, such as sex, and make it dirty and nasty that all kinds of bad things happen to the human mind:

Such as most pedophiles, and most serial killers, and voting Republican, and unwarranted suicides, and most mental illness, and unwanted pregnancies. (Teens not wanting to have sex is the perversion, not the other way around, and by replacing sex education and condoms, with unrealistic "abstinence", and by using blather about "low self-esteem" to shame them into not "sinning"—We have a teen pregnancy in the U.S. twice that of England and Canada!).

But none of this mattered, because their coffers over-floweth, and Hallelujah, it is a great day for the Lord!

There is a cure--------Tell our right-wing hypocrites, who Judge, rather than "Judge not"…. to shove it….

GOD

ABOUT THE AUTHOR: I was employed in our Criminal Justice System for a cumulative 20 years as a probation officer, with 5 of those years as a chief probation officer. I authored the concept of "Shock Incarceration" which became law in Kansas in 1970, and then was adopted in numerous jurisdictions in the U.S. and also spread to Europe—it is currently identified in the U.S. as "Boot Camp" [as the means to "shock" the young offender—and a total distortion of my original intent—like many ideas, once released, they take on a life of their own]. I also instigated establishment of the first Court Psychiatric Clinic in the U.S., in conjunction with psychiatrists from the Menninger Foundation, as a chief probation officer. Finally, I was the Democrat candidate for Congress, District 21, TX, 2000. I would most define myself as a Social Ecologist-- [albeit my degree is in Psychology]. My web page is

www.Inclusivism.org –which has been on the internet since 1996.
http://www.amazon.com/James-L.-Jim-Green/e/B001KHZIMM/ref=ntt_dp_epwbk_0

A BRIEF ADDENDUM: When the U.S. Supreme Court denied certiorari—where the violation of my constitutional rights were obvious, and criminal negligence on the part of the government defendants in the death of our son, equally obvious—[detailed in THE HARVARD BOYS CLUB, Amazon/Kindle]--I filed a Petition for Rehearing [which is automatic]—and included the following. The Clerk of the U.S. Supreme Court called me at my work in California, and asked that I withdraw the "cartoon" [a reprint from The NEW YORKER] from my Petition. I refused on the basis of the First Amendment, and it remains in the archives at the U.S. Supreme Court [Docket #: 79-1627], to this day. The wording [not that clear] is: "Excellent, excellent. A fine blend of truths, half-truths, and blatant falsehoods".

IN THE

Supreme Court of the United States

October Term, 1979

No. 79-1627

JAMES L. GREEN,

Petitioner,

VS.

"Excellent, excellent. A fine blend of truths, half-truths, and blatant falsehoods."

OTHER BOOKS BY THIS AUTHOR ON AMAZON/KINDLE/BN:

- THE HARVARD BOYS CLUB: Hitler's Assault On Our Freedoms From His Grave

- MY LETTERS TO PRESIDENT OBAMA: Confessions Of A Compulsive Letter Writer

- OUR GREED AND IGNORANCE: Poses A Far Greater Threat To America, Than Terrorism

- LETTERS ON STEROIDS: Confessions Of A Compulsive Letter-To-The-Editor Writer

- THE FIRST TIME I HAD SEX: And, The Religious Intolerance Attack On America

- WHY PRESIDENT OBAMA LOST THE 2012 ELECTION: A Wake-Up Call

- ECONOMIC INCLUSIVISM: Neo-Capitalism/An Anthology: Inclusive pro-market solutions to our social problems

- AMERICA IS ONE SICK MF: Why Greed-Driven America Went Off The Rails....

- EVERY GIVEN SUNDAY: A Scientific Formula To Predict NFL Games

And others….http://www.amazon.com/James-L.-Jim-Green/e/B001KHZIMM/ref=ntt_dp_epwbk_0